LifeBooks:

Creating a Treasure
for the Adopted Child

www.adoptionlifebooks.com

by Beth O'Malley, M.Ed.
(adoptee & 'older' adoptive Mom)

Published by
Adoption-Works
PO Box 520178
Winthrop, Mass. 02152
www.adoption-works.com
800 469-9666 (toll-free)

Copyright ©2000, 2001, 2002, 2003, 2004,
2005, 2006, 2008 Beth O'Malley M.Ed
ISBN 0-9701832-7-1
Library of Congress control number 00 091008
1. Adoption   2. Family   3. Adopted children

Printed in the United States of America

First printing July 4, 2000
Second Printing March 18, 2001
Third Printing July 18, 2001
Fourth Printing February 14, 2002
Fifth Printing June 22, 2002
Sixth Printing March 18, 2003
Seventh Printing March 18, 2004
Eighth Printing April 15, 2005
Ninth Printing May 1, 2006
Tenth Printing January 1, 2008

Original cover artwork by Ms. Susan Winget
www.wingetart.com
Editors: Sarah Jane Swart,
Technical assistance: Joyce Kelly
Original artwork "My Chinese Mommy"
by Cassie McGuire, age six

Also by Beth O'Malley M.Ed

My Adoption Lifebook: A Work Book for Kids from China
My Foster Care Journey (a foster and/or adoption lifebook)
For When I'm Famous: A Teen Fost/Adopt Lifebook

Ordering/Contact Information
www.adoptionlifebooks.com
Beth O'Malley
617 846-6718 or 1-800 469-9666
PO Box 520178
Winthrop, Mass. 02152

Table of Contents

Special Thanks

I never planned to write a book. Somehow, this book took on a life of its own; it became my baby. Its creation was fueled by the fact that I was on a mission—a mission to help adopted and foster kids feel good about adoption issues...or at least better than I felt growing up. Maybe having a few more pieces of information than I had could help lessen the pain that is sometimes associated with being adopted.

Since I'm not an official writer, I had to get lots of help with my book. Special thanks to my very patient and funny husband, Douglas Bell; Corinne Rayburn, for her life-saving wisdom and support; Deborah Wingard, for teaching me how to reframe anything; and Roberta Rosenberg, who found my first book on the Internet.

Can't forget my brilliant editor, Sarah Jane Swart. Sarah has the eye of an editor and heart of an adoptive Mom. Special thanks to Dr. Joyce Maguire Pavao, an adoption pioneer, who took the time to carefully review this manuscript.

My thanks also to Susan Winget, my talented and generous cousin, whose artwork has transformed my book cover; and my sisters-in-laws Catherine Trembicki and Janet Corbett, for their graphic art skills and encouragement.

I am forever grateful to Cathy Stucker, for helping me with her amazing ideas as I struggled in the early days. (You wouldn't believe my lack of confidence.)

You know, this book wasn't actually my baby. Instead it helped me find my baby, to become a mother. It's a long story—maybe another book.

I love parenthood. Becoming and being an adoptive mother have changed my life. If you want to hear more, there's a place where I talk about not only the new-to-me world of parenthood but also the world of lifebooks, and how and why these two worlds meet. It's my website, where visitors can sign up for my monthly newsletter: www.adoptionlifebooks.com/signup.htm

Take care,
Beth O'Malley, M.Ed

1.

INSPIRATION FOR YOUR LIFEBOOK JOURNEY

People often ask me, "What is an adoption Lifebook?" My first thought is that a Lifebook is the best gift in the world for an adoptee. It should be required for each adoption, just like the birth certificate.

Then I get serious and reply, "A Lifebook is a collection of words, photos, graphics, artwork, and memorabilia that creates a life record for a child who was adopted. It is a simple, truthful story written through a child's eyes."

A Lifebook is a security blanket, a concrete tool, and a medium for one complete personal history. It promotes positive grasp of identity, so it front-loads for adolescence. It makes talking about adoption feel like everyday conversation. It promotes attachment.

"…my daughter's Lifebook only brought us closer and increased her trust in me."
–Mary McGuire, adoptive parent of 7-year-old Cassie, adopted from China

A Lifebook is more than a life story. It is a unique opportunity for parents to honor every minute of their children's lives. It is the single most meaningful piece of "paperwork" that any social worker can complete. And foster parents? You can give an adoptee or foster child a sweet childhood memory.

I have witnessed the magic of Lifebooks firsthand and can testify to the powerful normalizing effect that these simple books have. In addition, I was adopted as an infant myself and helped raise my adopted niece Elisa from El Salvador. I'm able to combine personal and professional knowledge in my approach to the Lifebook. I believe that this combination enhances my understanding of Lifebooks.

Lifebooks help connect children to their histories and beginnings. They create foundations that help children attach to their adoptive families. For some children in adoptive situations, feelings of numbness and floating are noted when describing "not feeling a part of." Anything that quells these feelings helps improve quality of life.

A Lifebook starts with the child's birth, not their arrival into their adoptive family. It is completely focused on the child's experience and child-friendly facts. It is written in basic action words that a child can easily interpret when s/he acquires reading skills.

As you read through this book, try not to select just the sections that apply to your child's adoption. You may get ideas for pages or wording from unexpected places. In years to come, go back and reread different sections. Some will take on new meaning as your child grows older.

"…my Mother is a social worker who now uses Lifebooks in her work. I wish Lifebooks were available 22 years ago…maybe I wouldn't have so many unanswered questions."
–Kate Giblin, age 22, adult adoptee from Colombia, herself a new social worker

A. A Lifebook Is the Best Gift

It's important to recognize the beauty of a physical tool. The Lifebook can stay on a shelf or it can be brought down at will (control is always big with us adoptees). The Lifebook is a **visual reminder** of the adoptive family's validation of the child's existence, from the second s/he was conceived.

The Lifebook provides *constancy*; it doesn't disappear one day (unless somehow it gets lost in the house). Initially a parent can control the information and the way the story is presented. Then the book should be available for the child to be in charge of.

If s/he doesn't want to look at it until s/he graduates from college, that's fine. Adoptees know their Lifebooks are always there in case they need to know more or simply touch the pages. That's part of the security a Lifebook offers.

"…Joe's Mom died in a fire. He came to live with me at age 7 and stayed until he was 12. I always make Lifebooks for my kids. I made a point of getting photos of his mother from his maternal grandmother before she died. These were the only pictures he had of his mother.
"Some tough problems arose and Joe left quickly when he hit adolescence. In a huff. Angry. Refusing his Lifebook or even a picture of his mother. So I held onto it—for 7 years, to be exact. Joe finally returned and was ready for his Lifebook. He was 22, getting married, and having a baby."
–Bill L., foster parent

If you are an adoptive parent, imagine your daughter at age 13, sitting up late at night, going through her Lifebook. Or the glow in your son's eyes as he reads about when he first entered his family. Quiet, special times. What if this Lifebook gives your child the edge in terms of quality-of-life issues such as *intimacy?* What if the Lifebook magic could help hold them through difficult young-adult times? I believe it can. I hope you share my vision.

"…my 16-year-old son is a good kid. We adopted him as an infant and have always been open with him with what little information we had. Recently I read Lifebooks: Creating a Treasure for the Adopted Child. *As a result, one night I brought my son's adoption papers out, and I said he was welcome to look through them. "No thanks, Mom." But the next night he decided to take a look. Some little pieces of information took on new meaning, like his birth mother being the exact age he is now. That evening, [he said to me,] "I love having you as my mother." I responded, "I love having you as my son!""*

—Cathy, adoptive parent

Lifebooks give the family an attachment ritual: sitting together, reading the Lifebook. "Honey, do you want to get your Lifebook?" "Mom, I want to read my Lifebook.

Children (and parents) will know the words by heart. This process says, parent to child, "there is nothing I can't tolerate about your history." Lifebook talk becomes symbolic of adoption issues discussion. But no one ever said this would be easy.

"…my five year old son knows the words in his Lifebook by heart. As he becomes older and can comprehend more, the words will take on a new meaning. He will never have to "be told" and will always know that it's not his fault."

—Karen, adoptive parent

Families can either end the Lifebook at the finalization or add on throughout the child's life. The Lifebook has the potential to be ever changing. The child and family could later add in pictures, photographs, or even postcards from favorite teachers. For example, a child could include pictures of pets, original artwork, school awards, hobbies, etc.

B. The Best Way to Make a Lifebook

The best way to make a Lifebook is with the child. I can't stress how important this is. If a child is only two or three, they can participate by selecting the album type, picking out favorite photos, and doing some page decorating. From an early age, they will know about 'their special book' and the adoption story. As the parent, you are now completely comfortable with adoption language and questions. Everyone gains from a Lifebook.

"…one of my families adopted a baby [and] began Lifebook work right away…Now at age one he can pull himself up and seems to point to his Lifebook… naturally cooing, laughing, and making appropriate baby sounds… their relationship and his adjustment has already benefited."
–Celia Robert, social worker

If you are making a Lifebook for an infant, then leave some of the pages blank for when they are older, age 4 or 5. Artwork is the child's contribution for many pages where no pictures exist.

Feeling very ambitious? Then finish reading this book and consider ordering Special Report #4 Babies & Toddlers for my latest thinking and suggestions (see page 96). Adoptive parenthood has expanded my thinking in this area.

Always make two copies of the Lifebook. The original photos/pages should be carefully stored away to avoid pizza stains or angry moments. The color copies allow for your child to hold on to the Lifebook and use it on a day-to-day basis.

As I did Lifebook work with children or heard stories from parents, I soon realized that it was the small bits of information—like a favorite color, stories about the other children in the orphanage, what clothes they wore at the first meeting, or memories of a smell that helped ground children in their pasts.

This freed them to chase their dreams for the future. It wasn't always the major or official pieces of information that made children smile.

"...My adopted niece Tasha suffered significant abuse while living with her birth family. When Tasha was 12, her mother and pediatrician were successful in finding her hospital of birth and sent for her records. Tasha saw a page with her birthmom's signature. "We make the T the same way!" She was thrilled to find this unexpected connection...despite the abuse history."
–Carol, adoptive aunt

A *warm fuzzy fact* such as this one goes beyond the official record or 'hard facts' to enrich and enliven the child's story. These facts become the anchors of a child's memory and Lifebook pages.

C. 500 Words for Adoption?

The process of writing and reading the Lifebook helps familiarize the adoptive/foster family with adoption language. Whenever anxiety is reduced in adoption, there is a chain effect. The child picks up on the ease surrounding the topic and thus feels at ease.

Unless you work in adoption on a daily basis, words like *birthmother, birthfather,* and *birthday mom* don't pop up at the dinner table. The parent has to model use of these terms so they sound and "feel" normal for both the child and the whole family. Social workers need to do the same thing for the adoptive parents.

For most international and transracial adoptions, keeping the adoption 'quiet' is not an option. Intrusive questions come fast and furious, since the public is so curious when they see families with varying shades of skin color. Grownups and children alike always seem to want to know, "Is that your real child?" or "Or is that your real mother?" Working on Lifebook issues and language is a great way to prepare.

Are there 500 words for snow in the Eskimo language? We need to expand our vocabulary for adoption in order to have ordinary conversations. It's easy to get stuck if you call your child's birthmother only by her first name.

Here's a list of some names I've encountered:
- Birthmother, birthmom
- Birthfather, birthdad
- Birthday mom,
- Bellybutton mom
- First mother
- Chinese, Russian, Korean mommy
- Biological mother
- Lady whose tummy you came out of
- First name, as in "Karen" or "Momma Karen"

People may get stuck in referring to the birthparent as "real" or "natural." Acknowledge that there is nothing unreal or unnatural about adoptive parents!

"…my son['s] teacher was discussing mothers and families, so my son volunteered that he was adopted…One of his classmates asked, "What's that?" So he explained. The little girl [responded], "That's terrible, you don't know who your real mother is." "What?" my son exclaimed, "I live with my real mother." When he arrived home and shared this story, I told him, "Touch me. Don't I feel real to you? We are all real."

–Lyn, adoptive mother

Once the language is comfortable, then the structure provides safety, and within that structure adoption is easy for families to talk about. Each time you start to discuss hard birthparent information, you don't have to reinvent the wheel. It's all written down in the Lifebook. The words are in place to be used again and again, as explanation or as a foundation for discussion.

Tools for Normalizing Discussion of Adoption
- Lifebooks
- dinner table adoption discussion
- casual comments
- comments about famous people who are adopted

Did you know that Dave Thomas, founder of Wendy's Restaurants, is adopted? Or Olympic gold medal-winning figure skater and cancer survivor Scott Hamilton? Country singer Faith Hill? Rock stars Debbie Harry (Blondie) and Liz Phair? Author Mark Twain?

People who were raised either by relatives or in foster care include Eddie Murphy and Tom Monaghan, founder of Domino's Pizza. Would you be surprised to hear that rapper Ice-T, John Lennon, James Dean, Cher, and Marilyn Monroe also lived with relatives or in foster care?

And then there's Daunte Culpepper, NFL superstar and Minnesota Viking. Plus Charlotte Ayanna, actress and Miss Teen USA of 1993. And, of course, Dave Pelzer, best selling author—on the NY Times Best Seller list three times! Visit www. fosterclub.org for more detailed biographies. This is a great site for anyone involved with older kids and teens who have lived in foster care.

Not only does this make it alright to talk about people who were adopted or in foster care, but it also adds a certain glamour and excitement. These are cultural heroes that many children imitate. The fact that they are adopted or spent time in foster care is reflected glory for any adopted or foster child.

My favorite line is that *Superman was adopted.* Loading children up with positive adoption facts is one part of the attachment process over which you do get to exercise control.

You are about to give the adopted child a priceless gift—a personalized Lifebook! As you embark on this journey I have some questions for you:

❑ Are you interested in preserving precious childhood memories?

❑ Would you like to increase your child's self esteem?

❑ Do you want to create an heirloom passed down to future generations?

❑ Are you ready to take advantage of years of professional adoption experience and my instincts as an adult adoptee?

If the answer is "Yes" to any of these questions, read on.

2.

THE UNIVERSITY OF LIFEBOOK

I started my social work career more than 22 years ago. In 1994 I began working with foster children of all ages as an adoption social worker. My job was to prepare them for adoption and to identify permanent homes. One critical piece of this process was helping to create their adoption Lifebooks.

My first Lifebook was inspired by a 3 year old with the AIDS virus. Her birth mother was still alive, but signs were present that she would not live for long. Almost certainly, this toddler would live long enough to have questions: "Do I look like my birthday Mom?" "What was her favorite color?"

As a novice adoption worker I faced many challenges:
- learning adoption language
- processing pounds of paperwork
- making life decisions for children
- losing sleep over worry about finding matches

Out of all my different tasks, putting together a child's Lifebook seemed the hardest. But I had a lot of help. I had several excellent teachers who believed in the value of Lifebooks. In addition, having been adopted myself, I am able to combine personal experience with professional knowledge in my approach.

As you read along, I will talk about assorted benefits of Lifebooks, why Lifebooks are essential, roadblocks and creative ways to get past them, and my own story as an adult adoptee and adoption worker.

In this edition, I have included personal anecdotes from a broad assortment of people. Individuals from all over the United States have shared inspiring stories with me, largely due to my Lifebook workshops and website. To ensure privacy, I have changed names and in most cases refer to adoptive and foster parents by their first names only.

A. What Makes A Lifebook Priceless?

Adoptees often have few facts about their early lives. Since the adoptive family often wasn't part of the birth or earliest moments, there is no shared experience to discuss. Adoption expert and therapist Corinne Rayburn, LCSW, LMFT, says, "There are no carriers of history for the adoptee, as there are in birth families."

By reading the Lifebook, an adopted person can find words and pictures that help make sense of his or her life. An adoptee will have something physical, the Lifebook, that s/he can hold. In turn, the Lifebook will hold together a life story, validating an individual's rich and varied memories and experiences. The Lifebook becomes the "carrier" of history.

Concrete tools for holding that history become vital when the adoptee's name changes, the courts change the adoptee's birth certificate, the adoptee loses his or her first mother, and s/he doesn't look like anyone in the adoptive family.

Little-Known Lifebook Facts

A Lifebook provides
- A concrete tool for meaningful conversation
- Increased comfort level for adoptive or foster parents in adoption conversations
- An adoption security blanket
- Attachment rituals
- Structure for difficult material (such as reasons for the relinquishment)
- Ways to normalize adoption language
- Ways to reduce fantasy about birthparents

- A front-load for adolescence
- Opportunities to create positive identity and ethnic identity
- Space for future events
- Reduction in divided loyalty conflicts with birth family
- Ways to confront and change magical thinking

B. Magical Thinking

Adopted children often have secret thoughts about why they were adopted. Many believe that somehow they are responsible for the separation from their birth family.

Children with histories of abuse and neglect usually take it further. They somehow believe that they are responsible for being separated from their birth families.

"…one 5-year-old boy had been sexually and physically abused at an early age…I explained to him that there are thousands of children who aren't able to live with their biological parents, that all the reasons have to do with mothers or fathers having grownup problems…I went on to describe, in child terms, examples of neglect, physical abuse, sexual abuse, and good and bad drugs. After several home visits, I finally asked him why he thought he was no longer with his birth mother. His response: "Because I was bad?"

–J.B., social worker

This is the power of magical thinking. Remember the children's rhyme, "Step on a crack, break your mother's back"? Children believe that they are the center of the universe and so very powerful. Maybe they were moved because they wet the bed that night…the damaging speculation is endless.

It is always a good idea to ask your child directly why s/he thinks s/he is no longer with the birth family. This is true for both domestic and international adoptions. Even if you have

19

already told your child his or her adoption story, it bears checking out, and the truth always bears repeating.

Claudia Jewett Jarratt supports this notion in her book <u>Helping Children Cope with Separation and Loss</u> (a classic for talking to children about loss and change; I learn something new every time I reread it). She says that sometimes helpers worry that a child is too fragile or young to discuss a loss. "Unfortunately such well-meaning avoidance in a helper leaves the child alone with his fantasies…and these are often more frightening, self blaming, and damaging than the actual facts would have been."

Lifebooks help reduce magical thinking and fantasy. They free up an adopted child to pay close attention in school, or to be fully available to focus on talents and interests. Better for a child to be out playing soccer or painting a picture than to be fantasizing endlessly about "what happened."

If your child comes from another country, be aware that it's important to discuss the country's conditions and/or rules for adoptions. Often this is the only explanation a child has as to why s/he was placed. Lifebooks are the ultimate teaching tool and they can **save hours of therapy** later in life.

Lifebooks help answer questions, increase self-esteem, and teach children the truth. They are the ultimate teaching tool. Sometimes children create their own histories, which may not be correct. By creating Lifebooks with them, you can help to gently offer more accurate pieces of the story.

"…as I was doing a teen's Lifebook, she kept on asking, "Why didn't I stay with my mother?" I researched her question. It turned out that, despite day visits, there was never a time when she had actually returned to her birthmother. Lifebook work allowed for the opportunity to help correct wishful fantasy[,] which had turned into memory over the years."

–Carolyn Goodrich, social worker

C. Waiting Families & Lifebooks

Good news for waiting families: pre-placement is a perfect time to start the Lifebook process. Before children arrive, parents will have *time*—a luxury not often enjoyed once children are at home! Use that time to

1) keep a journal,

2) pay attention to non-critical information,

3) maintain alertness to the 'warm fuzzies,' and

4) gather information, through examining history and through interviewing people involved in the placement.

One great way to start is to begin a journal. ODS Adoption Community of New England, Inc., Executive Director Joan Clark says that keeping a journal helps both process your own emotions and record vital pieces of information.

Journaling permits us to rely on our experiences, not our spotty memories. The adoption process can be lengthy and stressful, not unlike pregnancy. Holding on to an assortment of events, names, and hard and soft facts is next to impossible when you can't remember where you put the car keys some days. If you keep a journal, that journal will always be available for review.

Another way to start is by simply maintaining attentiveness. This is related to keeping a journal, because sometimes connections between events aren't made right away. Parents may receive pieces of information that don't fit neatly together. Only over time, after repeated exposure, do the pieces of the puzzle suggest where they might fit.

In addition, synchronicity (unusual coincidence) seems to pop up a great deal in the adoption world. Sometimes these connections seem to be a million-to-one; they just call out, "This is unbelievable!" Reviewing a journal can help facilitate making these connections—but first we have to be sure we're paying attention to the details.

M

"A couple adopting from Russia was planning to follow their religious tradition of naming their new baby after a grandmother who had passed on. . . . Often people choose either the first name or the first initial, which was M in this instance. When they received the referral papers, the baby's first name already started with M, and she was born the same day that the grandmother died."

—as told to ODS Adoption Community NE Executive Director Joan Clark, adoptive mother

These stories contribute to family history and honor a spiritual dimension. They enhance the 'legend' quality of the adoption story, giving children a sense that this was always meant to be. This sense may enhance positive feeling and help with acceptance of adoptive-family values, once the teen years arrive.

A third way to start the Lifebook process is to maintain alertness to 'warm fuzzies,' which are pieces of personal, family-oriented information that are not typically part of the official record. Waiting parents can be sensitive to warm fuzzy facts as they engage in such pursuits as travel to birth countries, meetings with birthparents to discuss open adoption, or receipt of foster care placement information. As you move through the adoption process, developing Lifebook 'antenna' for cute items and other tidbits will help you collect the stories your child will cherish someday.

One of the best times to soak up information—the fourth means of beginning a Lifebook—is prior to placement. Once placement occurs, then the initial attachment period sets in. Sometimes this period isn't compatible with examining your child's birth history, placement history, or the reason s/he became available for adoption. (This is why it's best for foster children to be placed in adoptive homes with up-to-date Lifebooks.) I often find that after placement it takes 12–18 months before the Lifebook journey can be resumed.

Before placement occurs, search out those pieces of information that will turn to gold in the teen years, even during young adulthood. As the 'Lifebook detective,' see this search as Job 1! The information you uncover will help lay the cornerstones of your new family's foundation.

Often, as a child becomes older, s/he will have numerous questions about the pre-placement period or birth family history. These might be as simple as, "What was the name of my favorite staff member at the orphanage?" or direct and complicated, such as, "Is my birth mother still alive?" During adolescence and early adulthood, adoption information takes on great significance.

Personally, I always hated doctor visits, when I had to say I knew nothing about my medical history. Medical information can be difficult to obtain, yet few things are as necessary to have. Pieces that may be just as vital to track down are nuggets like the birthmother's favorite childhood games.

Try to interview people who had contact with birth family members. Treat the orphanage staff as extended birth family. Get quotes about your child, the full name of the person quoted, and photos. Open adoption? Don't be shy—find out as much as possible about the birthfather, his childhood interests, talents, nationality, personality traits, favorite things. Do the same for the birthmother. Treat each opportunity as if it were the last, because you simply never know what the future might bring.

Lifebook information comes to you via official documents, your recollections and experiences, and the results of paying attention to new types of information.

D. Roadblocks to Lifebooks for Adoptive Parents

Despite the importance of Lifebooks, often months turn into years and the photos remain in the drawer. A Lifebook is very difficult. I bet you know this—it's why you bought this book! Lifebooks are time consuming, anxiety provoking, and often overwhelming, plus there are no deadlines.

What happens is that parents want to make Lifebooks, but life keeps happening and the guilt starts to mount. Also, there is the enormous emotional energy it takes to balance out what information should be told and when.

In my Lifebook consultations, I often encounter those tricky adoption secrets, which tend to sabotage Lifebooks. There are pieces of information that some parents really don't want to ever share but know in their hearts they must. These translate into those dreaded "secrets."

"…my son has two older bothers still living with the birth mother. I haven't told him about his brothers, since I don't want him to feel badly [about being] the only child placed for adoption."
—adoptive mom

If you are a parent and feel strongly about a particular issue being more appropriate later, don't let that stop you from starting a Lifebook. You don't have to share everything at once. But hear me out in terms of reasons to be open from the start:

#1 It never gets easier. The longer you wait, the worse it feels.

#2 You run the risk of someone else telling your child the "secret."

#3 Your child picks up on your guilt.

#4 By sharing all the facts early on, it means that you never jeopardize your child's trust in you.

Lies can damage trust and relationships in such a way that it takes years to repair, if ever. If you wait for adolescence to share facts such as other birth siblings, your child can look at you and ask, "What else haven't you told me?"

There are situations, especially with siblings, where there are multiple issues. Try and carve out just the fact that your child has a brother or sister and consider sharing just that information.

> "…there were allegations of incest with the maternal grandfather in the family of origin…my son may be tied to that incestuous relationship in ways I'm just not ready to deal with… I have not told him about his siblings, who probably know."
> —adoptive parent

It's not necessary to initiate contact or do more than talk about the existence of a sibling. Do not confuse Lifebook work with search or reunion. Merely introducing the information that birth siblings or birth family exists does not necessitate developing a relationship.

It is your responsibility to create boundaries that provide emotional and physical safety for your family. Do be prepared, however, for these possible questions: "Can I meet her?" "Why doesn't she live with us?" "Can she come and live with us?" Take a deep breath and say, "Not today," or whatever your truth is on that subject.

You never know how certain facts will be interpreted by a child. S/He might find it very comforting to know there is a birth sibling somewhere in the universe. The adult translation is, "How sad that must make you feel." But who knows?

> "…there were twin brothers who had been separated at birth. One was the model child and the other was always getting into trouble. It just so happened that they lived in towns in the

same state. During adolescence the 'good' twin managed to travel to his brother's town and was arrested due to his brother's outstanding arrest warrant. He kept saying, "But that's not me," and of course no one believed him, since they were identical. What a way to discover you have a brother."
—as told to J.T., social worker

I recommend staying with the truth, always answered at the child's level. Count on any misrepresentation to come back and haunt you. Keep in mind that we all have a story and are entitled to know our histories.

Don't give up or put this off. This will be one of the best gifts anyone will ever give to an adopted child. I promise. However, when social workers, foster parents, or parents stop long enough to really take in an adoptee's story, it can be a painful experience. It's much easier for adults to focus on creating a new life, at the expense of leaving a child's roots buried deep.

To work on making a new family is certainly critical, but it is a mistake to wipe out or whitewash a child's history. Corinne Rayburn, veteran adoption therapist says, "Remember that these children have lived through the events." Ms. Rayburn (or St. Corinne, as some call her) also points out that you can hold and nurture a 5 year old as s/he grieves part of the adoption experience. When a child is 15, it's much harder to hold him or her in your lap.

"…if anyone had bad luck it was Sam…He had close to ten placements in his 12 years of life…several disruptions not related to him…one adoptive father died, while another committed suicide. He had 9 older siblings living all over the state. I was nervous about doing his Lifebook, wondering if it would make things worse[,] but I knew how much he needed it. After reading his long Lifebook, Sam asked, "Is that it? That's not so bad!" Putting it all down on paper made it so much more manageable for him."
—Veronica Fiscus, social worker, Nevada

Children seem to have a natural way of not hearing information that is too hard for them (so do adults, for that matter). This can take the form of not hearing "clean your room" or include more serious adoption issues.

"…one little boy staunchly disagreed with some of the information in his Lifebook. My solution was to add the true version starting with, 'But my social worker says it happened like this.'"
—Veronica Fiscus, social worker

As the parent, foster parent, or social worker, you can only say the words, which may very well not sink in at that time. The point is to plant the seed—or actually seeds. The seeds need replanting at each new developmental stage. (Just as you're thinking: now that we've gotten past that one…)

E. Creative Interventions for Social Workers

Social workers have the dilemma of having too many emergencies involving life-and-death situations. Lifebooks are quality-of-life items that don't amount to emergencies. No one ever died from lack of a Lifebook.

However, the outcomes of substance abuse and depression can be dire. Lack of attachment can result in relationship problems, alienation, emotional numbness, and subsequent social symptoms. This quality-of-life item matters a lot if it's **your** life.

The list is long of reasons why social workers don't complete Lifebooks. But I have a few suggestions for ways social workers can get the process started.

To begin, try simply capturing some information about the birth parents that isn't in the case record. Interview any social worker or foster parent who may have met the child. Get a physical description. Jot down any impressions and thoughts these people may have.

Take all this information and put it into a manila folder labeled Lifebook Stuff. Include some pictures in the folder, at least one of the child whose Lifebook is in process and one of the birthparent or -parents. Birthparent photos are a timeless gift— can you imagine never knowing what your mother looked like?

Date the photos. Give them a picture of yourself. Put in a copy of the birth certificate (check your state's regulations). Ask them to draw a self portrait. Include the child's height and weight, dated, at the bottom. Make a copy of a report card and include it.

Interview the child and create a list of their favorites: Favorite TV show, dessert, friend, activity, etc. Write this out on a piece of paper with the date. Photocopy his or her hand print.

Ask the foster parent to write a funny story, no more than one page, on something that happened in their home. Request a picture of that home. Go back and take a picture of a foster home where the child lived. Write to former foster parents and ask for photos.

"…I developed a form letter and sent it out to all of Sandy's 8 foster placements. Within two months I had 3 photo albums filled with pictures. What a gift!"
—Lyn Liphart, adoption specialist, Georgia

"…the pediatrician sent out form letters to every hospital in the area to find out where my adopted niece was born. Bingo! We got lucky."
—Carol, adoptive aunt

Maybe the foster parents enjoy scrapbooking. Ask them to read the section in this book on the difference between scrapbooks and Lifebooks. See if a foster parent is interested in making pages for the Lifebook. Interview them in terms of nicknames, family rituals, favorite friends or family members who visit…special meals or vacations.

It is this type of information that often only a foster parent knows and can pass on. A gift of a lifetime.

Perhaps in the future, foster parents will be more involved with the Lifebook process. *Lifebooks ideally need to be built though a collaboration among foster parents, social workers, therapists, adoptive parents, and the child.*

F. My Own Adoption Journey

As I worked with foster children, I began to have questions about my own story as an adoptee. Was I born in a hospital? What did I look like when I was born? What did my birthfather look like? And what did those doctors have to say after I was born?

I remember being 18 and going to the City Hall to get my birth certificate for my driver's license. They didn't have it. I had to publicly announce, "Well, maybe it's because I was adopted" at the counter. I nearly died.

I went home and sobbed to my mother that I didn't have a birth certificate. She answered, "That's because you weren't born here in this city. You were born clear across the state. We thought it would be easier for you to just say your hometown was your birthplace." She wanted to make my life easier, bless her. (Bless her for all that she has given me.)

With that single piece of information—my birthplace—I think that lights flashed and the whole world shifted for me. I found out where I was born. What a grounding experience.

Never underestimate the power of information. Adoptees are able to process and make sense of those facts that are theirs, that belong to them. It's the not knowing that becomes so difficult.

G. Birthparent Fantasy

I used to wonder what happened to my first mother. In fact, I imagined a scene in which she died immediately after giving birth to me. Then, in another scene, I envisioned both birthparents dying in an airplane crash. At about age 8 I stopped the fantasies and just envisioned a large, blank movie screen.

Fantasy is a large piece of the adoptee's emotional world. Lifebooks help shift thinking to more concrete and reality-based concepts. Less energy is expended on "wondering." Lifebooks also help provide answers where there are gaps. Solid facts mean that children can spend more time paying attention to teachers than on wondering why their birthmothers didn't want them. Of course, some children and teens have more glamorous thoughts:

"...I made Lifebooks for both of my children. My daughter's book ended up in the living room. I encourage her to continue to add on, and occasionally I check in on her newest additions. How else would I know that she thinks Cindy Crawford is her birth mother?"

*   –adoptive parent*

3.

ESSENTIALS FOR LIFEBOOKS

A Lifebook is very different from a picture book or even a scrapbook. Vera Fahlberg, M.D., in <u>A Child's Journey Through Placement</u> (with an excellent section on Lifebooks), describes the differences as consisting of the following:

- the Lifebook always starts at the child's birth
- it mentions the birthmother and birthfather
- the reasons why the child was adopted are discussed

A Lifebook allows a family to not only record precious facts but also to **capture memories** for the child as the Lifebook is made. In fact, it is likely that the child will recall the process as much as the information at various times of life. The Lifebook is an invaluable tool that families increasingly appreciate as their children grow older.

I have made infant Lifebooks with several families who have stayed in touch with me. Now these families are reporting that their children are proud of their Lifebooks and can talk openly about their histories. The children often take the Lifebooks out and show them to family members and close friends. They want to add on with their new pictures and stories.

"Dear Beth; We recently received a copy of your book and were honored to find a symbol of our family within its pages…We cannot express how excited we are that other adoptive families will have an opportunity to share in such a wonderful and necessary experience. Their children will forever thank them for it…embracing the truth has made our family very close and able to overcome anything that might come our way."
—Sandy Jones, adoptive parent

A. Triple AAA for Lifebooks

We know the benefits of Lifebooks and how tough they are to put together. What's a parent to do? What do you do if you have adopted and there is no Lifebook and no tidbits of childhood information? Here are some thoughts.

Look around you. I'll bet that you know someone who is good with the computer or writing, maybe a friend or a relative. Talk with them about doing some bartering. I'm sure that you could devise a sweet exchange of services. Give them this book to read and then sit down with them for about an hour.

The next step: Say good bye and let them write an outline for the Lifebook. Sound good?

Another idea is working with your child's therapist, if s/he has one. This is a time-honored tradition among many adoption workers. Therapists who are adoption competent are excellent resources for Lifebooks. You may also consider getting a therapist strictly for this purpose for your child.

What about a friend to serve as a Lifebook coach? Again, share this book with them over coffee. Devise a 10-week plan, with a commitment to write one page each week. Each week you meet to review the page. It helps to have emotional support and a reachable goal.

Do you know several families who need Lifebooks written? Try "trading" children. If you write a Lifebook for someone else's child, the emotional baggage almost disappears.

What about starting a Lifebook support group through your adoption agency? Look for Lifebook workshops popping up all over the country. Checkout my website (www.adoptionLifebooks.com) for lists of workshops. Attend adoption conferences, which often have Lifebooks sessions, for inspiration.

What about the hundreds of photos you have taken since day one? Don't tackle them alone. Get your sister, husband, partner, girlfriend, etc., to assist you. Select 8 to 10 photos. Focus on the youngest baby picture, referral picture, " birth country" photos, and pictures of foster parents, foster siblings, social workers, birthfamily, day of arrival, and court finalization, plus one favorite family picture.

Organize the photos into envelopes with a theme for each one. Record on the envelopes which time period they contain. This just helps keep you on target with the pictures. Again, include your child in the photo selection if s/he is old enough.

I do recommend, as a first choice, that the parent write the Lifebook. But I am a realist, and I know that life and circumstance will not permit everyone to do this. In this edition, I include full-length examples for domestic and international adoptions. Feel free to use the text and simply cut and paste your child's personal information.

B. Memory Books

There are a number of hardcover albums with special pages, called Memory Books or Memory Albums. These are ready-made, fill-in-the-blank books. In my opinion, one major difference between memory books and Lifebooks is that memory books don't read like stories. The memory book does feature space to add your child's and family's personal information and pictures.

Here are some questions for assessing memory books:

What type of graphics or pictures are included? Are the children representative of different ethnic groups?

Do the questions focus on the parents' memories vs. space for the children's facts? Remember, a Lifebook is the child's story.

Is this book suitable for international adoptions? For open adoptions? For foster care situations?

Does the language work for single parents or other non-traditional situations?

Does the Memory Book include a page for information on birthparents? This is critical for any type of adoption. In a Lifebook, for example, that page might say, "We know nothing about your birth father. Not even his name." But stating that we know nothing is so important.

C. Scrapbookers & Lifebooks—A Shift in Perspective

With just a few changes and a small shift in perspective, a scrapbooker can create a Lifebook with ease. After all, scrapbookers are already familiar with laying out pages and with spending focused time on each page. The major differences between Lifebooks and scrapbooks are as follows:

♦ A Lifebook contains only truth; a scrapbook can contain fantasy.

♦ A Lifebook is private; a scrapbook is eagerly shared.

♦ Lifebook pages revolve around information; scrapbook pages revolve around pictures or artwork.

♦ It's recommended that the child be included in creating the Lifebook; scrapbooks are often made solely by the adult.

♦ A Lifebook has set essentials; a scrapbook thrives on different themes.

The first change is that scrapbooking traditionally features happy memories and fantasy. Although there have been articles on "healing pages" in scrapbooks (Memory Makers Magazine, July/August 2000, #19), usually the pages of a scrapbook are vibrant with splashes of positive feeling.

In Lifebooks, what is featured can bring on sadness as well as positive feeling. Birth family and placement information, sometimes including abuse and trauma, is hard for most Lifebook writers, and especially for adoptive parents. The writer needs to really believe that the child will ultimately benefit from hearing or reading information that historically (approximately 1940s to 1980s) was 'tucked away' for when children were 'older.'

"The Lifebook is the truth, the whole truth and nothing but the truth, as opposed to the scrapbook, which contains fantasy and the good, giggly, and bubbly…"
–Nola Stewart, adoptive and foster
parent, avid scrapbooker

Another difference is that Lifebooks are private, whereas scrapbooks are "for show." It is up to the child when and where they share a Lifebook (with ultimate parent veto power, of course).

The lesson about privacy vs. secrecy is very important and can't be offered vigorously enough. The Lifebook is a family book; the information isn't for show-and-tell. It's not a secret— secrets can be toxic, and the family is not ashamed of any of that information. In fact, the family is sensitive to and accepting of even the most difficult information. It is *private* because only a child's intimates need to know all of that child's 'business.'

Teachers, for example, might need to know that a child is adopted, so as to frame lessons without compromising the adopted child's identity or performance (and it may be necessary to pro-actively address some mythology about 'troubled' adopted children). Teachers, even the best teachers, probably *don't* need to know a child's birthfather's name. Try to think of Lifebook information as being available on a 'need-to-know' basis.

Let's review Lifebook basics:

- ♦ A Lifebook begins at the child's birth
- ♦ It always includes information about the birthmother and the birthfather (if you don't know anything, state that you don't)

♦ It explains the reason for the child's placement (be it conditions of the birth country, an adoption plan based on choice, or abuse/neglect)

♦ If there is a history of pre-adoption placements, it includes any information known, including reasons for leaving placement/s

Again, in Lifebooks, information is central. Pre-placement photos are often nonexistent; then they overflow once your child arrives. The temptation is to work with the beautiful pictures you have on hand. Keep in mind that the words are just as important as the pictures, if not more so.

Journaling becomes critical because it is the only way to blend together those periods with tons of photos and those periods without. It's possible to have many pages of words with only attractive borders as 'art.' The effect is one of creating mental images for the adopted child. Your words create pictures where none exist.

"...I realized I needed to include more of those 'little things.' I [needed] to do more journaling."
–Sandy Parker, foster and adoptive parent

Words should be not only child-focused but also appropriate developmentally. When deciding what to include, ask, "Would my 4 year old be interested in this?" Center each page on the child.

A shift in perspective is that one of the best ways to make a Lifebook is with your child. If the child is an infant, leave space for future add-ins—don't delay getting started. But if your child is old enough to participate, then include him or her in many Lifebook choices. For example, s/he can help select the album, stickers, or pictures.

This is a perfect time for children to make drawings for those periods without photographic documentation. For international adoptions, children can clip pictures from magazines of their birth countries or of customs, dances, foods, and toys they particularly enjoy.

If your child is creating art for the Lifebook, the best way to include it is to get it laser-copied. Otherwise the crayons, chalk, etc., may eat away at the pages of the Lifebook.

Finally, some scrapbookers suggest that Lifebooks, with their pre-set recommendations, tend to be more formal than scrapbooks. Some of the pages contain only borders and words! It has been said that the journaling is so great in a Lifebook that in some ways it resembles a fancy diary.

I think of it as an honest and loving biography.

D. Kids Like Me

True confession time! If you haven't guessed it already, I am not very 'craftsy' (but greatly admire anyone who is). Within the past 1-2 years, scrapbook companies have devised new papers, borders, pre-cut photo mounts all designed to save time and keep things simple.

Did I mention that my Lifebook journey rekindled an old love of stickers? I have an extensive collection and am always looking for new ones. One of my best discoveries is a series called A kid like ME™, by the company Me and My Big Ideas. (Special thanks to Stephanie Rahmatulla, whose idea became a long overdue reality.)

Now available are Asian American, Multi-cultural, and African American children sticker sheets, in addition to brunets, redheads, and blonds. These are available at several websites, such as www. scrapandtell.com and www. stickerplanet.com, for about $2 per sheet.

This may sound like a commercial, but in reality it reflects my excitement about new resources. When hard-to-find or unique materials that can be used in Lifebooks are available, I want to shout it to the world.

E. Writing the Lifebook

Lifebooks are a lost art form, like hand stitched doilies or hand made quilts. They require both emotional energy and practice. In the following section I have included comments for adoptive parents, foster parents, and social workers. Please use whatever applies to your situation.

Modern life is so busy with music lessons, therapy, work commitments, and family events that taking the time to sit down and put your child's life on paper gets lost in the shuffle. It is not a crisis. There are no deadlines. After all, who has the time?

"Well, I do," you answer. "Otherwise I wouldn't be reading this!"

"OK," I answer, "are you ready to make a commitment?"

Look at the calendar and give yourself a drop-dead date for completing your child's Lifebook. It's OK to be fairly generous—perhaps 2-3 months. Don't start this process if you're approaching the holidays or an upcoming major life event, such as moving or starting a new job. But then again, there are always unexpected situations, so be fair with yourself and your child.

To help you with this process, I offer a monthly Lifebook Tips newsletter. You can sign up for it on my website at www. adoptionlifebooks.com/signup.htm . It arrives in your email box. After you sign up for the newsletter, a series of "lifebook lessons" will start. Also for free. Since you're reading this book, most of the "lessons" will serve as a review.

The newsletter is different. Not only will it be your only official reminder to get going—but it contains new ideas, articles, contests, and a ' personal section.' Sign up now before you forget!

Writing Suggestions
- ✓ short, colorful pages
- ✓ child facts versus parent facts
- ✓ strong visual focus for each page
- ✓ use actions words and dialogue
- ✓ be funny—forget about grammar
- ✓ brainstorm if stuck
- ✓ consult with peers and friends for input

Keep each page short and sweet. The tendency is to put in too many details when you begin. There is a clear danger of turning a Lifebook into an adoptive parent's journal. I call those details 'parent facts,' versus child facts.

For example, a parent fact is describing how you felt meeting your child versus what the child looked like. Keep in mind, children are egocentric and caught up in how life currently affects them. They may have limited interest in events prior to their birth until they are older.

"…doing a Memory book with my 13-year-old daughter, she looked at me and said 'that's your memory, not mine.' By going through the process, I learned what was inside her."
—Lyn, adoptive parent

It's easy to get lost and let pages get long—too long to be read on a regular basis, and too long for your child. One way to combat this is to read each page out loud. That gives you a natural guideline on length.

Something I've experienced while reading Lifebooks as a social worker is that the young child is preoccupied with the pictures and wants to flip through the pages. It is thus important to have only one graphic or photo on each page to try and keep them visually focused.

Use short, simple sentences. Don't get caught up in fancy adjectives. Try **action words** and **dialogue** wherever possible. It makes it much more readable and "real" if there are actual quotes. Use words for sounds, like the bees **buzzzing** in the spring. Don't hold back. For example, "Your father thought that you looked like a prune when he first saw you."

Hold on to your sense of humor. The material is so emotionally intense, I think keeping a sense of humor in Lifebook work is critical. Make it light and funny where appropriate. Besides helping you with your sanity, it brings smiles when you or other adults are reading it.

If you get stuck on a page, give it a title and then jot down words associated with that event. Don't get caught up in the perfect term or in judging yourself. What is most important as a memory? Put the page away and give it some time. Give yourself permission to simply mull things over and not have an answer right away.

Title Page

Start with a title page. Let the child pick the photo if possible. I always use the child's picture to begin the Lifebook. As you can see from the back cover, I never get tired of my baby picture. (I think it's an adoptee thing.)

Page 1

I call this the "birthday page." Describe the season and include typical activities and/or favorite family events. Then, perhaps, ask if they know why their birth date is a special day.

Dr. Joyce Maguire Pavao, author of <u>The Family of Adoption</u> and Director of the Center For Family Connections, says, "To an adopted person without a story of their birth, there is the thought that maybe they are not *like* all other people. Always tell something about birth."

Fall is a wonderful time of year. The leaves start to turn colors. Children go back to school. Families think about the holidays.

But something even more special happened on September 4, 1977. Jade, can you guess what that is?

Someone you know very well was born on this day.

You! Jade Bell!

Page 1

Page 2

This is the actual birth page. Discuss where the child was born, name the hospital, provide birth weight, and discuss whether s/he was healthy or not. What time was s/he born? This information is usually located in the birth certificate. I often ask questions in relation to the time of birth, like the question in the example.

For international adoptions, Page 2 often has scant birth information. Dr. Maguire Pavao emphasizes the importance of always including birth information despite how little you have.

I like to include the meaning of the child's birth name. Especially in Korean and Chinese adoptions, the birth name seems to represent beautiful images: spring and sunflower, for example. These represent excellent opportunities for colorful graphics, child's artwork, or magazine pictures (and natural ways to increase self-esteem).

Cathy, you were born in the Guangdong Province of China on April 2, 1994. Your Chinese name was Guo Chun Kui. It means "spring and sunflower."

What a beautiful name, Cathy. Strong and shining. Can you draw a picture of your name?

Page 2

Page 3

In the beginning section, always include a copy of your child's birth certificate. Children love seeing this official information. It is a source of great delight for youngsters and "grounding" for older children. It also insures that accurate information is passed on.

Be sure to explain the social/legal reasons for the "false" birth certificate. It can be odd for older adopted children to look at their birth certificates, knowing that they had different mothers at birth, yet seeing their adoptive mothers' name on the paperwork.

A 9-year-old client informed me that he thought his birth date moved up a day each year. He had lived in three foster homes in the previous three years, each of which had a record of a different date. I had to show him his birth certificate to prove his birthday.

Page 4 is the "Where did I come from?" page, which discusses the birthmother and growing in her tummy. Select language that you are comfortable with in terms of the birth. Some parents will want to introduce anatomically correct terms, such as *uterus* or *birth canal.* Others will use the *tummy* term, which gets the point across, but some will argue that this term isn't correct.

> Everyone in the world starts by getting born. You, too!
>
> Before you were born, you grew in a special place inside another lady's tummy *[use a first name if you have it]*.
>
> Joyce helped make you. We call her your "birthday mom" or "first mom." *[Or you can say, "That lady is someone we call your Chinese Mommy."]*
>
> Page 4

A point of interest is that I had one foster child argue with me that he wasn't born. There is so much information that is naturally passed down in families but gets lost in the foster care system.

When I sit with foster children and parents and talk about babies growing inside tummies, I may pull out my shirt and exaggerate what pregnant women look like. Everyone laughs, and the child understands.

Research indicates that children become capable of understanding some of the simple aspects of reproduction by the time they are 4 or 5 (and are aware of skin color differences at age 3). Children have all seen expectant mothers and can grasp that idea.

Page 5

This is the "Facts of life" page, which discusses the fact that it takes two people to make a baby. Actually, it takes a birthmother's and a birthfather's genes.

It takes two people, a man and a woman, to make a baby. Everyone in the world starts with a birthmother and birthfather. You, too. So not only do you have a birthmother but you have a birthfather as well!

Page 5

Pages 6 and 7

The next several pages will be for birthparent information. This is one of the most powerful aspects of Lifebook work, because you have an opportunity to instill favorable images and ideas of the birthfamily.

On the birthparent pages, use actual pictures if available.

Your birthmother, Susan, was born in New York. She was 16 when she gave birth to you. When you were born, Susan liked to play the piano and write poems. Her favorite color was yellow.

[Include a photo if possible!]
Page 7

I do caution you to be very careful with whatever type of graphics you use. Don't use graphics with pictures of anonymous people, since this is how your child will recall their birthparent. Better for them to draw a picture than for a Lifebook to instill false images. At this point, you are creating memories. These are critical pages and words!

If you have birthfather information, then write something like, "Your birthfather's name is Jack. He is 5'6", has brown hair, and is Italian. He went to high school and really liked to work on computers there."

If you have no information, then say, "We don't have any information about your birthfather. We don't even know his name. But I bet you can draw a picture of what you think he looks like."

We don't know very much about your birthfather. In fact, we don't even know his name. I wonder if he likes animals the same way you do, or if he likes to play computer games!

Since you have never seen what he looks like, why don't you use your imagination and draw his picture?

Page 6

Please don't wait to talk about birthfathers. Children often figure out that a piece is missing. Silence gives the message that this is somehow a source of shame.

In addition, if you know it, always write down the nationality of the birthparents. This is very important as children process normal issues around identity.

Your Chinese mommy gave you your looks. She would have the same color hair and skin as you. I wonder if you look like her. Since we don't have a picture of her you will have to imagine what she looks like. Be an artist and draw a picture of your Chinese mommy.

Page 7

I want to emphasize that these are the pages where you can imagine that some of your child's talents might be related to what the birthparents were like. I call this "adolescent front-loading" in Lifebooks, a new concept. I first heard the term *front-loading* at the Center For Family Connections.

Dr. Joyce Maguire Pavao, founder of the Center For Family Connections, describes it as "doing the work in the beginning and then filling in the developmental spaces, instead of 'waiting' to do things later, as the time is never right."

I had one case in which the birthmother was an excellent dancer and loved to sing. It turned out that the little girl also had these talents. Her adoptive mother was able to say that she found out the birthmother shared these strengths. This seemed to help the child not only feel good about her but also develops a positive fantasy of her birthmother.

You want to plug in many areas of strength so that the adoptee has a vision, which lends itself more to Olympic ice-skating then quitting school or smoking pot. The Lifebook is a unique opportunity to build strengths.

If you had only five pages for your book, the birthparent section should still be the longest. It gives children a chance to explore and express their birthparent fantasies via artwork or actual pictures. Parents, foster parents, and social workers can assist children with seeing positive connections to their pasts and weaving together disparate pieces of their lives.

I realize that for many adoptive parents this section is extremely difficult, especially if there has been a history of abuse. If you get stuck, try some suggestions in the Triple AAA section. You might want to gather some friends who "get" adoption issues to support you in completing the Lifebook.

Throughout the adoptee's life, s/he will hear about the day s/he arrived into the family. The stories abound from that point. The child's birth and birthfamily don't naturally get discussed because family members often weren't included. The Lifebook helps to fill that void.

Page 8

If this is an international adoption, the Lifebook presents a natural opportunity to include interesting pieces of information on the child's birth country. Think child-friendly facts like food, games, special clothes, native animals, and music. What do children enjoy doing in that country?

If you have an older child, I insert a page to say, "Cassie's Favorite Things About China," or "Interesting Things About Cassie's Birth Country of China," and then write down what she says. It's also a wonderful art opportunity, or magazine pictures and original photos can be cut and pasted.

Page 9

Now for the "Why was I adopted?" page. This is where the child is told the truth about why s/he isn't with his or her first mother. (It gets easier after page 9, I promise.)

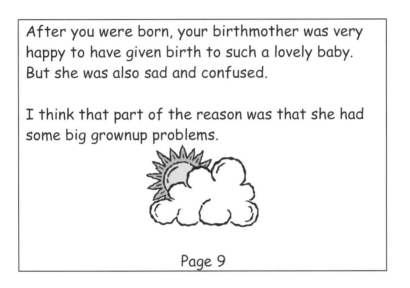

> After you were born, your birthmother was very happy to have given birth to such a lovely baby. But she was also sad and confused.
>
> I think that part of the reason was that she had some big grownup problems.
>
> Page 9

Discuss the reason the birthparent couldn't take care of the child. Emphasize adult responsibility. Children tend to think they cause everything and that somehow things are their fault. Keep stating that it wasn't your child's fault. Also, if it's true, explain that the birthmother couldn't care for <u>any</u> child, not just them. This information can boost self-esteem and help an adoptee combat potential negativity.

I also believe that it's "safe" to speculate in your child's Lifebook that the birthmother was feeling many different emotions after giving birth. You can discuss feelings such as sadness, happiness, and confusion. Use the words "I think that..." or "I'll bet..." Once again, it helps the adopted child to talk about the initial loss both for the birthmother and for themselves.

Adoption is such a celebration for the adoptive family that it is easy to fail to pay proper attention to the fact that each adoption starts with a major loss. Corinne Rayburn, LCSW, LMFT, and adoption therapist of 20 years plus, calls this the "bittersweet" of adoption.

Giving young adoptees the opportunity to acknowledge their grief (even if they don't feel it) helps ground them in the future, particularly for when they become teenagers. The well of sadness does not have to sit and collect, only to seep out during adolescence. Try and do as much frontloading as you can for teenage years.

After children are born, they either live with their birthparents or move into another family or orphanage. There are many reasons why children don't stay with their first mother and father.

All the reasons have to do with the parents, not the kids. Little babies can't do anything wrong. How can they? They are just little goo goo ga ga babies.

Page 9

The **Page 9 example** is the most general language that I would use. It is best to be more specific. Remember to think through each message. If you say, for example, that the birthmother was sick, then every time you become ill, the question "Will I have to leave now?" arises for your child. For any international adoption, discuss the situation in the country that led to the conditions around the adoption. For example, in Korea and Russia it is very difficult for unmarried women to raise children.

> In your birth country it is very hard to be a single mother. It can be hard on the baby and even a young child as s/he grows. Your birthmother was worried that this would cause big problems for you. Kyung-Sook made a very painful decision.

In Russia it is "not proper for a woman to be in an intimate relationship with a man unless they are married or close to being married," says native Russian Marina Senderovich, a U.S. Adoption Specialist. She says, "For some young teens they feel it is *better to die*. These teens often leave home in an effort to hide their pregnancies."

Young unmarried mothers travel to larger cities with maternity wards in the hospitals. These mothers do everything possible to conceal their names and origins. Information about birth fathers is unavailable in most cases.

But Marina is quick to share that, during an Armenian earthquake disaster (1980s), the neighbors and extended family came forward and cared for all the orphans to prevent them being adopted by strangers.

Overall, adoption is very secretive in Russia, as evidenced by the following story.

"…Katrina wanted a baby very much. She made arrangements through her friend, who was a gynecologist, to have the baby of a young teen mother placed with her. This is very illegal. Katrina went through 'morning sickness' and gradually became bigger as if she were pregnant. She went into the hospital the same time as the teen mother; the baby was placed into her arms as if she had given birth to him. All the time Katrina and her husband lived with Katrina's mother in a one-bedroom apartment. The grandmother never knew her granddaughter was 'adopted.'"
—as told to Marina Senderovich, native Russian, adoption specialist

Major problems such as war, not enough food, and drug or alcohol addiction are easier to understand than, "Your mother couldn't take care of you." Adoption will make much more sense to a child with concrete explanations for placement. If this is an older child adoption, then they have experienced the trauma and have survived.

Try to be as specific and visual as possible when giving the reason for leaving the biological family. For example, there is a big difference between telling a child that his or her foster mother in Peru was too poor to keep him or her, on the one hand, and saying, on the other hand, "Your foster family didn't even have money for food. They had to go to the ocean when you were two months old and fish." The images are very different.

If poverty is the stated reason, always discuss the differences between the United States and the birth country. Be clear that in El Salvador, for example, birth families don't have access to ATM machines or credit cards. Being poor doesn't mean not having money, it means not having food or clothes.

"The rich people in the United States should send money to El Salvador. That way, the poor birthmothers can keep their babies."
—a suggestion offered by a 6-year-child adopted from El Salvador

The theme that every child needs and deserves basic care is universal. It's a parent's job to feed the baby, buy diapers, and find good babysitters. Babies are supposed to be fed and safe.

Dr. Joyce Maguire Pavao says that a major piece of the work lies in parents discussing with adoptees the economic, political, social, and religious pressures that resulted in the adoption.

With girls from China, Dr. Pavao reframes the notion of "abandonment." Dr. Pavao talks about the birthmother being creative by purposely placing her child in a public place to be found and cared for. Their placement becomes an act of love.

However, she adds that adoptees will be unable to understand the abandonment from the birthparents' perspective until they are able to think abstractly, around ages 12–13. A key task for adoptive parents is building positive self-esteem in adoptees so that they have the inner resources when the time comes that they feel unwanted or personalize the rejection.

Page 9 Why Was I Placed? is also where you will need to tailor the information according to the child's age or developmental level. Experts have very different opinions on this matter with regard to how much detail. You must decide for yourself—you know your child best.

If you have an older child who lived in foster care, then this will affect word choice. These children have "lived through it." It helps them when their parents organize this information and put words to the experiences.

Dr. Gregory Keck, Ph.D.—Founder of the Attachment and Bonding Center of Ohio and co-author of Adopting the Hurt Child —says that sometimes they have to "rewrite childrens' Lifebooks" at his center. He says that "social workers sometimes sanitize" them. Children can say to themselves "Oh well, it wasn't that bad." And yet it was.

When children have suffered really horrific abuse (e.g., were sexually used or deliberately burned by a birthparent), they need to know that this was in fact a terrible thing that happened to them.

Being direct and clear about the abuse history can help later in life if the child wants to glamorize his or her birthparent. Memory is a funny process, which can get foggier as time goes on. Lifebooks keep everyone honest, which especially helps during adolescence.

Examples for explaining abuse and neglect:

[Substance Abuse] After you were born, I'll bet that your birthmother was very happy to have given birth to such a lovely baby. But it sounds like she was also sad and confused. I think that your birthmother was worried because she had some big problems. One of her problems was that she used bad drugs. Now, you know that there are good drugs and bad drugs. Good drugs, like penicillin, are prescribed by doctors to make people get better when they are sick.

People take bad drugs like cocaine or too much beer to make themselves feel better. So, a person might feel happy or silly for a little while and forget about their problems. Later on, bad drugs always make people feel even worse.

[Depression] Your mom felt sad a lot throughout her life. When this happened she would stay in bed and sleep. Nobody cleaned the house or went to the store for food. Sometimes, no adult was watching you to make sure you didn't get hurt. It must have been hard for you to watch your mom sleep so much and be sad. The sadness was not your fault. Part of your mom's brain needed special medicine that a doctor prescribes to help her feel less sad. I wonder if your mom knew about this. It sounds like your mom needed special help to feel better. There was nothing you could have done to fix her.

[Physical Abuse] Your first social worker told me that your father used to hit you with a belt and leave marks on you. Sometimes he got so angry that he didn't stop. I bet it really hurt.

There are lots of reasons why grownups aren't supposed to beat kids. What are some of the reasons that you think? Let's make a list.

♦ grown ups are supposed to keep kids safe, not hurt them
♦ grown ups are bigger than children—it's not fair
♦ adults and kids are supposed to use their words, not their hands, when they get mad
♦ kids are supposed to make mistakes; it's an adult's job to teach them new ways

[Sexual Abuse (with thanks to therapist Susan Lerner)] Boys and girls sometimes have touching troubles. This can be bad touching or secret touching.

56

Bad touching is something that happens to everyone. It's when your sister smacks you too hard, or someone pulls your hair, or you get hit by someone who wants to hurt you.

Secret touching is when a boy or girl is touched on his or her private parts by someone. Private parts are the parts of your body that are covered when you wear a bathing suit.

After this adult or big kid touches you, then they make you promise not to tell anyone and that it is a secret. They scare you by saying they'll do mean things if you tell. That is secret touching.

In **Domestic Identified Adoptions**, I believe that you need to discuss why the birthparent made the adoption decision. It's not enough to say a birthparent "made an adoption plan." The unspoken question is "Why? Was the birthparent young? Without enough help to raise a baby? Why didn't they want me?"

[Young Parents] Your birthmother and birthfather were very young when you were born. They could barely take care of themselves. It was too hard for them to also have a baby. They still wanted to be teenagers.

[Siblings Still with Birthfamily] After you were born your birthmother was very happy to have given birth to such a lovely baby girl. But she was also very sad and confused. Sarah had some big problems. She didn't have very much money and there was no one to help her take care of another baby. You see, Sarah has two other children, Tommy and Peter. They are your birth brothers.

Sarah felt that it was all she could do to take good enough care of your birth brothers. One more baby seemed just too hard. So she made an adoption plan. She didn't know you as a person and didn't give you this plan because of you. It was because she knew that *she* could not be a good parent to another child. She wanted you to have parents who were able to take care of you.

It's easier to work with the known, even for young children. Otherwise, one can get lost in daydreaming about what might have happened. You can add on more details when they get a little older and can have more compassion for their birthparents.

Pages 10 and 11

These pages are focused on the planning. Name the adoption agency and social worker involved. Talk about signing papers to make a voluntary plan. This helps the child understand that she wasn't "taken" or "kidnapped" and that the birthmother wasn't coerced—a real concern for some adoptees, according to Dr. Pavao.

If there was court involvement, then discuss who the Judge was and his or her role. Sometimes it helps to explain that originally a social worker was sent to visit the house to watch and make sure that the children were safe. Children often remember their social workers—but don't assume anything.

> After you were born, your birthmother needed extra help to take care of you. A social worker visited your house to watch your family and make sure you were safe. After many visits, the social worker decided to write a letter to the Judge about your family. She told the Judge, "I'm very worried."
>
> A judge is a man or woman who is a very smart and wise person. People go to a Judge and explain their problems. They ask the Judge for help with decisions. The Judge decided that you needed to live in a safe place called a foster home.

["**Planning" page example:** The following is one of my favorite "inspirations" pages in my personalized Lifebooks. This page can be used for both international and domestic adoptions.]

Your birthmother worked hard to make your adoption plan. I think she had a nice dream for you, which you and your family can talk about later. What do you dream about doing when you are older?

Page 11

Orphanage/International (Pages 12+)

These pages should give as much detail as possible. Be sure to include this page even if the placement was for a day. Use as many pages as necessary for this period in your child's life. For international adopted children, this information is the closest to "birth family" info the child will receive.

If you are planning on traveling to pick up your child, remember to get staff members' names and photos. Try to get actual quotes about your child when they were in the orphanage. Get pictures of the crib, where they took baths, in addition to the facility pictures. Ask permission to take pictures of other babies in nearby cribs. Find out names.

What type of food was served? Was there anything your child seemed to especially like? When were meals served? What kind of soap was used for baths or washing clothes? Seek out the details of your child's everyday life.

Bring back copies of local newspapers, and take pictures of McDonalds or cans of soda reflecting the birth language. Get a small plastic bag and fill it with earth. Hold onto outfits and don't wash them, to preserve the smell. Video tape as much as possible.

For domestic foster care examples, please see the next section, entitled What About Foster Parents?

Page 13 Coming Home

You are heading into the home stretch. The Lifebook foundation has been laid, and it's time for the fun stuff—the day your child joined your family! Now the stories and pictures abound and result in those magic moments: "Tell me about the day I came." Storytelling is so comforting to children.

[Coming Home Example—International]

Finally it was time to go meet you at the airport. All the parents were waiting in this big room. You were the very first baby who came off the plane. All dressed up in a pretty yellow outfit. And you know what? I knew it was you before they even called your name.

[Coming Home Example—Domestic]

The first time your father saw you, you were very quiet and lying in your crib. He picked you up and tossed you in the air. Whoops! You opened your mouth and out came breakfast all over Daddy's new tie. We all laughed. I think we still have that tie.

C. What About Foster Parents?

Foster Care (Pages 12+)

If your child is school age, then this is a perfect chance to help tease out memories of foster homes. Find out who else was in the home at that time. Grownups tend to minimize the importance of foster siblings, who are as significant to the foster child as any relation. Find out who were favorite people in foster care.

> *special nicknames, activities, hobbies, pets, foods, neighbors, schools, family members*

> *cooking smells, foster siblings, religious activities, type of neighborhood (rural, city), household rituals*

> *how the foster parent's voice sounded, type of punishment used*

On January 12, 1998, your social worker picked you up in her red Toyota and brought you to your first foster home. Vroom, vroom!

Auntie was at the door waiting and James was watching TV.

When I searched for history via my old case record, my favorite piece of information came from my first foster family. They told the social worker I "smacked my lips" as a baby and "the whole family laughed." I'll never forget my lip-smacking story. It is my favorite piece of information.

Susan Harris, M.S.W., an affiliate of the Center For Family Connections, describes foster care as the "holding period." She continues by saying the "holding period is a time that often has no recorded memory, no voice, and no name—a time span that is considered so critical yet so often unknown by many adoptees and other persons who spent time in foster care."

If your child spent time in foster care or has a trauma history, then I strongly recommend that this Lifebook work be done in conjunction with a therapist. Not any therapist, but an adoption competent therapist who can help integrate the losses and assist you emotionally, as well.

In my adoption worker experience, I have seen that an older child is able to draw pictures of events from conscious memories—such as domestic violence and parental drug use—for the Lifebook. This is part of the healing process for the adoptee who has lived through foster care. It was painful for me as a social worker, so I can't quite imagine how it would feel for the adoptive parents.

Overall, creating the Lifebook with the older child is invaluable because it increases trust and attachment. Children trust that their parent/foster parent can tolerate their pain from the past and help them work through it. They don't have to take care of their parents in this area.

With any child, including those in international adoptive placements, there is the possibility that s/he will experience behavioral regression (behavior associated with younger ages) while working on the Lifebook. This is normal, but you should be prepared. Consult with an adoption competent therapist if this becomes a concern for you. The rewards—behaviorally and emotionally—do appear later on.

If the child lived with birthparents, then these memories should be included. Artwork can be very helpful. Ask the child to draw a picture of his or her recollections of the birth home. When going back to early times with birthparents, include happy memories. Give your child the space to discuss enjoying some time spent with birthparents.

Giving permission to discuss birthparents helps reduce the divided loyalty a child might feel. Divided loyalty is a powerful emotion that detracts from attachment in the new family if left unattended.

I recall working with a young girl who had been abandoned by her birthmother two years previously. As part of her Lifebook work, she was able to draw pictures of a birthday party when her mother rented a pony. These were some of the happiest times of her life, despite the neglect she suffered. It was a learning experience for me as her social worker as it challenged the stereotypes I had in mind about the birthmother.

Foster parent contributions to Lifebooks are so necessary. Whether they actually write the pages or compile cute-kid/cute-baby stories, foster parents have insights that are invaluable. The results of adding these insights can be like turning paper into gold.

Over the years, as I have read through old case record notes, the absence of child specific comments was always striking. Traditionally, many case notes are directed toward terminating parental rights. Consequently, the most damaging information is highlighted. Simply finding the time to write case notes has been a challenge for most protective social workers, myself included.

The result? Many beautiful stories about the children whom foster parents care for end up lost forever. Adoptees lose another piece of their life, because we weren't able to figure out—as a system—how to incorporate the stories. Let's change that.

I'm going to assume that, as a foster parent, you are very busy. Is that a safe assumption? And I'm going to ask you to take on more work—without payment. Doesn't that sound just like a social worker?

But I know that **what you really want** is to give your foster children a chance at a decent life. Lifebook "stuff" is one of the few concrete tools that is a *certainty* for improving a child's life. You are giving them their childhood memories. What could be more important than that?

I love the story that I found in my foster care notes. It makes me smile and gives me peace in my heart. I feel connected to the universe and to myself whenever I picture my baby self in the foster home smacking my lips and everyone laughing. (Susan Harris created the phrase "baby self.") This is my only story from that period.

So I have a couple of ideas. **Number 1 is the Memory Box:** Take a shoebox and wrap it in pretty gift paper. Wrap the cover separately. Do this every time a child enters your home. Make it a welcome ritual. If you don't like to wrap, ask a friend or relative or buy a pretty tin at Christmas Tree Shoppes or a similar bargain outlet.

The reason for the gift-wrapping is two-fold. First, foster children often have such unattractive rituals as garbage bags instead of luggage. The wrapping makes it pretty. Secondly, it's

65

to remind you that you are giving this child a gift every time you write a memory and slip it in the box.

Start with notes about the type of things that you think will never get recorded in the case record. Jot down a page when the child enters your home. *Make sure that you sign it and date it.*

Keep the box someplace easy to access. Put in a few school papers, report cards, locks of baby hair, baby teeth, etc. Ask your foster child to remind you of things. At various times put down a few more notes. Imagine what would be important to you 10 or 20 years later in life and which mementos increase in value over time. Think about what you would like to know if you were an adult and had no information. This will become the gift of a lifetime for your foster child. They will never forget you or your generosity in creating this box for them.

"…my adopted niece Tasha has a memory box. By age 12 she has created an entire ritual of taking out her treasure. It clearly gives her so much comfort."

–Carol, adoptive aunt

Speaking of not knowing, can you imagine going through life without ever knowing what your mother or father looked like? Foster parents often have the unique opportunity to get photos of birth parents. Foster mother Sandy P. shared the following story:

"…I took three-year-old David for a visit with his birthmother while she was incarcerated. They didn't allow cameras inside the facility. Shortly thereafter she was released, overdosed, and died. So I learned a lesson. At the next visit with a different child I took pictures. If his birthmother dies abruptly, he will know what she looked like!"

If you plan to write the Lifebook, then follow the outline as described earlier. Do whatever works for you, in terms of either handwriting it typing it on a computer. I'm sure it will be beautiful. A few lines are terrific about the child's birth, birthmother, birthfather, and reason for coming into care. Copy the page suggestions directly from this book if you aren't feeling creative.

> "…Lifebooks remain important to my children. They show that their biological connections are still important and will never be forgotten."
> –Michelle Braxton, single foster/adoptive parent of seven

Before you begin, check in with your foster care social worker and the child's adoption worker (and therapist). We do work in a system where the more communication, the better. Ask the adoption worker for input if you get stuck or want feedback. Chances are they will be thrilled you are putting this together. If they want to write this Lifebook themselves, then give them those beautiful memory-box notes. The foster child can only benefit when we all work together.

If you aren't the first foster home, try to provide the dates of entry and departure from previous homes, plus the reason they had to leave, if this is known. If you are doing this with the child, try not to censor whatever they are telling you. Sometimes it can be pretty unbelievable.

Time will tell on whatever the issue is which came to light during the Lifebook. (If the child discloses abuse, you do need to share this information with appropriate staff at your agency.)

D. If Your Infant is now school age

What if you haven't gotten around to making a Lifebook and now your child is 6 or 7?

"One of the advantages of not having gotten around to making my daughter's Lifebook is that now—at age 8—she can play an important part of it."
–Mary Chris Bulger, adoptive parent of an 8-year-old girl from China

Age clearly plays an important role in determining how to present Lifebook work. Naturally, for infants and toddlers you will be doing all the work, leaving a few pages blank for future artwork.

If your child is over the age of 4, I suggest making this a major process. Get creative. Tweak interest, make it fun, and be consistent.

Introduce the topic by announcing that "it's time to start a Lifebook now that you're older." Create a mystique around the process. Set a date on the calendar and announce that this is when "we will begin to start Lifebook work." Take it all very seriously, and so will your child.

Your initial Lifebook date will be to buy the book. You can take a trip to a local scrapbook store or keep it simple at Michael's Crafts Store, AC Moore, or Staples. As you know, kids love stickers and will be in sticker heaven at a scrapbook establishment. Budget in advance.

One difference with an older child is that you might start with some warm up exercises. Read some appropriate adoption books. Have you adopted from China? I recommend <u>When You Were Born in China</u> by Sara Dorow. Get the juices flowing and warm up gradually to the adoption subject.

Start with current information. Have your child do a page on their favorites: favorite color, food, TV show, best friend, activity, etc. If this is an international adoption, then do a page on Favorites about their birth country.

Next, move on to baby pictures (or artwork) and how babies are made. A great book is <u>Contemplating Your Bellybutton</u> (by

Jun Nanao) for explaining the facts of life—tasteful but explicit pictures which help the child "get it" via the role of the bellybutton. The book <u>How I Was Adopted: Samantha's Story</u> (by Joanna Cole) explains the birth process as part of the adoption process in a fun, easy manner.

This sets the stage to work your way back to birth and subsequent life story. Be sure to allow kids to select the pictures that go into the Lifebook. It's a nice bonding experience to get out all those wonderful photos that are normally tucked away and go through them together.

If this is an international adoption, then little will be known about the birth. This is where you can use words like "I'll bet that..." or "What do you think you looked like when you were a baby?" and then write your child's thoughts. Be sure to state, "Susie thinks she looked like..." to differentiate between fact and fiction.

Grief and "stirring things up" are not uncommon with older children or with international adoptees. These are healthy reactions to major losses in their lives. Lifebooks allow them the opportunity to acknowledge their pain and loss and to share their feelings with you.

Remember Ms. Rayburn's words: "You can rock them to sleep as they cry when they are little." You must be able to tolerate your child's sadness as you go through the Lifebook process.

[Page example for starting with current information]

All About Me

I am ____ years old.

My favorite dessert is: _____

My favorite color is:_____

My bravest moment was

_____.

The school I attend is _____.

Suzie's favorite things about her birth country ...

I want to be a _____when I grow up.

Three things I'm really good   Three things that bug me:
at doing: 1
   1   2
   2   3
   3

Pocket Pages

How are you going to handle information about which you don't want the entire world to know, regarding your child's history? Everyone has his or her own ideas about what information should be "public" versus "private." Your child will tend to use the Lifebook as a way to share history. If you want certain aspects private, then I suggest "pocket pages" or "travel Lifebooks" or a "show-and-tell book."

As you write the Lifebook, put any topic only for family eyes contained on one page or two. You can explain to the child that although it's not a secret, it's a part of his or her life that is private, so teachers and school friends do not need to know. When it's time to take the Lifebook in for show-and-tell, simply remove the pocket pages.

Another possibility is the "travel Lifebook" or " show-and-tell book," which is a separate three-ring binder that contains favorite pictures and pages (copies) from your "master" Lifebook. These binders are created with nursery school, preschool, and school in mind. Purchase a binder with a slip-in plastic cover so that the child's picture becomes the title page. Children love this!

In past editions of my book I recommended NOT having two different books for your child. Now that I've adopted myself, I see that it is really impossible to have a single Lifebook. There is the child's private Lifebook, toddler Lifebook (if you choose), travel books, videos, framed pictures, etc. Not to mention the traditional family albums, starting after the Lifebook.

When are you done with the lifebook? Some families add a page each year at the child's adoption anniversary. Others stop at the adoption finalization or when their child 'comes home.' It's up to you and how much the child owns the process.

E. Full-length Lifebook Examples

The following section contains three full-length Lifebook examples: One international (China), one domestic infant, and one from foster care. These are stories I have created from anecdotal material and are not actual Lifebooks. I do try to put in authentic facts where possible, such as the White Swan Hotel in China.

Most situations are far more complicated than the examples I have included. The purpose is to give you the basics, start to finish.

Please read through each one carefully, and feel free to use any of the pages and/or wording. Naturally, you will want to modify according to the child's age. This text is written for a preschooler aged 4–6.

I do love stories and hearing about how families have used their Lifebooks. Please write to me at lifebooks@earthlink.net so that I can share your success with other families and keep us all inspired.

Also, I have added a new tool to help ' remind' and 'inspire' you about Lifebooks. It is a 7 day email course filled with my best tips. Sign up at www. adoptionlifebooks.com/signup.htm

Plus it turns into my monthly newsletter. This serves not only to provide you with fresh ideas, but a little reminder if you haven't completed the lifebook.

Creating a lifebook is a process. Your struggle to organize and write the text is therapeutic. It brings you to a new emotional level as an adoptive parent. Some people take months-others years to complete it. Just don't give up. Or rationalize that since you talk about the adoption, you don't need to do this.

Summer is a wonderful time of year. School is out. No more snow. Families go on vacation. The sun shines bright.

But something else very special happened one summer, on July 5, 1997. Carrie, can you guess what that is? Let me give you a hint. Someone you know very well was born on this day.

You!

Carrie, you were born in the Guangdong Province of China, on July 5, 1997.

Your chinese name was Guo Chun Kui. It means "spring and sunflower." What a beautiful name. You were born during the time of monsoons, or heavy rain in China. The rains helped the flowers grow.

Before you were born, you grew in a special place inside another lady's tummy. That lady is someone we call your Chinese Mother. Your Chinese Mother gave you your birthday. She also gave you your looks. You and your Chinese Mother would probably have the same color hair and skin. Carrie, why don't you draw a picture of what you think she might look like?

Carrie, it takes two people, a man and a woman, to make a baby. Everyone in the world starts with a birthmother and birthfather. You too. So not only do you have a Chinese Mother but you have a Chinese Father as well.

We don't know very many facts about him, not even his name. Some things we will just have to guess at.

I wonder if he liked school. I wonder what his favorite color is. Maybe it's the same as yours!

You can draw a picture of him on this page.

After children are born, they either live with their first parents, join other families, or enter orphanages. There are many reasons why children don't stay with their first mothers and fathers. All the reasons have to do with the parents or the birth country, not the kids.

Little babies can't do anything wrong. How can they? They are just little goo goo, ga ga babies!

Carrie, let's go back to your story. When you were just a baby, you were born in China. China is a large country that is very far away.

You would need to take an airplane to get to China. Maybe someday you will go and visit the country where you were born. Let's take a look at China.

China is a country with millions of people. It is very beautiful but also very crowded. Sometimes people have a hard time finding places to live and even finding food.

So the people in charge of China made a rule. They made the rule that mothers and fathers could only have one child or sometimes two. If you broke this rule, there were big punishments.

We don't know your Chinese parents' exact reasons for placing you for adoption. But we can imagine it was a very hard decision.

I'll bet your Chinese mother and father thought and thought about what to do. I feel sure that they didn't want to break the rules and get punished. I also feel sure that they loved you and wanted good things for you.

So this is what we believe happened: Your Chinese parents made a plan. They decided to put you in a place where they knew you would be found and taken care of. This is how parents in China make sure their babies get adopted.

Your Chinese parents couldn't change the rules in China. But they could make sure that you grew up healthy and happy, and this is exactly what they did.

A lady (we don't know her name) found you bundled up at the city park, outside a tiny farm village. Someone, probably your birthparent, had carefully pinned a note to your clothing. The note said what your name was and when you were born. The lady brought you to a big baby home, the Xin Yi orphanage.

But there's more. You may have seen a lot of girls adopted from China. Why do so many Chinese girls get placed for adoption?

In China, parents live with their sons until they die. If a mother and father are allowed only one or two children, it is important to have a son—someone to take care of them when they are too old to work.

If Chinese parents have only girl babies, they worry—just like Chinese parents who have more than two babies. Culture says that only boys take care of parents, but parents also love their baby girls. What to do? Placing baby girls for adoption is one answer.

The Xin Yi Welfare Orphanage was mostly a big baby home. But on one floor lived grandparents and great-grandparents who liked to hold the babies.

Inside the orphanage, there was a big room with lots of cribs. This is where baby aides would hold and feed you and the other babies.

Outside the orphanage were bushes and flower beds with pretty pink blossoms.

Page 13

While you were getting born in China, I was waiting for you in the United States. I went to Wide Horizons for Children adoption agency and talked to a social worker, Lisa Lovett. I filled out lots of papers.

Page 14

Finally, the Chinese adoption agency sent a picture of you along with some medical papers. When I first saw your picture, I thought, "She is so tiny. Look at her beautiful little mouth."

The papers said that your favorite thing was "getting held by the baby aides." I couldn't wait to hold you myself.

Page 15

Finally I got the call—it was time! I quickly packed my bags.

On September 8, 1998, I got on a plane headed to China, with other mothers and fathers. All of us were traveling to meet our daughters.

Page 16

After two days in the hotel and more paperwork, everything was all set. We went to your baby home. I got to meet the aides and other staff members who had taken such good care of you. I waited while they went to get you. They called out your name as they walked into the room.

There you were—eyes shining bright—looking right at me. I reached out and held you tight. You were finally in my arms. It felt so good!

I took pictures of everyone at the orphanage who had taken such good care of you. One woman laughed and said, according to translation, that you hated getting a bath and always tried to wiggle away!

Another young woman was crying and gave you a big kiss. She said you were her favorite baby and she would miss you a lot. (Everything seemed to happen so fast that I forgot to get everyone's names, but I *do* have an address.)

That night was our first evening together at the hotel. I didn't want to put you down for a minute. We played on the bed, and you laughed at my funny faces. It was like we had been together for years.

I made a little bed by pulling together two chairs, kind of like your crib at the baby home.

The next morning was harder. You didn't seem to like anything I tried to feed you. I think I smelled, spoke, and made foods completely different from what you were used to. But I was patient and made little food games.

Soon it was time for us to get on the plane with the other families. These would be your friends in years to come. I took more pictures and exchanged addresses.

We arrived in the United States on your grandmother's birthday. It would always be a double celebration for our family.

When we got off the plane, there was Grandma waiting with balloons and a teddy bear. Aunt Sue and lots of friends were waiting, too. What a wonderful day.

Page 21

On March 15, 1999, we visited Judge Lewis in the Worcester Probate Court. The Judge's job is to make sure that children are safe and taken care of.

The Judge asked me if I would love you and take care of you no matter what happened. I said, "Yes, Carrie is my daughter and I will always love her."

Page 22

So the Judge signed the papers, and you were adopted.

Hip-Hip-Hooray!

Here is your adoption-day picture.

Page 23

[Title Page—a perfect place for child input and creativity. Let the child pick the picture/s and help decorate.]

Summertime is a wonderful time of year. School is out. The sun shines bright, and—yum, yum, yum—can you smell that barbecue?

But wait . . . something very special happened one fine summer day, on June 21, 1993. Can you guess what that is? Someone you know very well was born. YOU! That's who.

You, Nicole Shauna Corbett!

Nicole, you were born at 11:53 PM on a Saturday evening. I wonder if that means you like to stay up late!

The name of the hospital where you were born is Melrose Wakefield Hospital.

Look at your baby picture. What a cutie pie. In fact, your nickname was Sweet Pea.

[Insert birth certificate.]

Nicole, when you were newly born, everyone said, "Look at how much hair she has!" Meanwhile, you were very interested in drinking your bottle. You would make this loud slurping noise every time you drank. Slurp, slurp, slurp—can you make that sound now?

Page 5

But now it's 2001, you are 8, and you are able to do lots of things. Let's make a list of your favorites things to do:

[Have your child list favorites, such as 'I like to draw,' 'I like to swim,' 'I like to help Mom,' 'I like school, 'I like to read.']

Page 6

And what about some of the things you don't like to do?

[Have your child list dislikes, such as 'I don't like making my bed,' 'I don't like going to bed early,' 'I don't like practicing piano,' 'I don't like eating cream of wheat cereal.']

Page 7

Nicole, let's go back to your beginnings. You began like everyone else did, as a special sort of egg that grows inside a woman. It takes a woman and a man, who fertilizes the egg, to make a baby.

Janet is your first mother's name. You grew in a special place inside her before you were born. All women are born with this special place inside. It is called a womb.

Kevin is the name of your birth father. He helped make you.

Page 8

80

Before you were born, your birthmother made the decision that she couldn't take care of a baby. She had two children already, Sam and Peter, and she didn't have anyone to help her.

Janet was worried she didn't have enough help or money to give you a good home. It was just too hard for her to do.

Your birthmother's decision was made before she met you, while you were still growing inside her. It was a very difficult decision, one that would change all our lives, forever. She thought very hard and cried a lot. Janet decided to find you a mommy and a daddy who would love you and take wonderful care of you always.

Janet went to an adoption agency called Friends In Adoption. She told a social worker there that she wanted to find a mother and a father who would love and take good care of her baby. The social worker told her there were many families waiting for babies. She said that Janet could pick the family she felt the best about.

Each of the families had made a special book with pictures that told all about them—kind of like a Lifebook for the parents. We had made one of these books. In it, we wrote that we liked to go to church and participate in family events.

Janet liked how we sounded. She told the social worker that she wanted to meet us.

I'll never forget the day we went to meet your birth mother. We walked into the office, and there she was! (You were there, too, growing inside Janet.) I thought to myself, "Will my daughter be as pretty as her birthmom?"

We talked for a long time, and I can't even remember what we said! Soon it was time to go.

As we got into the car, I felt so worried. What if she didn't pick us? Suddenly we heard a yell: "I want you to be my baby's mother and father!" It was Janet, calling out the window to us. She had already decided that we would be your family. Your father and I couldn't stop laughing for joy.

We met Janet once more before you were born. Let me tell you about her: She is 5'8", is of English and French heritage, and has big blue eyes. (Your eyes are just as big!) She has a good sense of humor and loves animals. When you were born, Janet worked in the hospital as an aide. Her favorite color is yellow. When she was little, she had a white fluffy dog. Janet told us that she loves to eat lobster rolls from Kelley's at Revere Beach. Will you be a fish lover?

Your birthfather's name is Kevin Sommers. He is the man who helped make you. We didn't get to meet Kevin, and Janet didn't have a picture of him. But she said that he is "very smart, likes to draw, and graduated from high school." Your birth father is of Scottish and Irish heritage. Janet described him as a "handsome man."

Soon it was time for you to be born. Your father and I were both in the delivery room. Janet was working really hard to help you get born. Suddenly we could see your little head, with all that hair—and we heard a loud cry right away. Nicole, you were saying, "Hello, world!" in baby talk.

You were a healthy baby. The doctors gave you an A+ on the baby report card.

Page 17

In just a day it was time to say goodbye to Janet and hello to your forever Mom and Dad!

Here at home, your room was all set up with little Winnie the Pooh curtains and a cute little musical lamp. But first, you stayed with Mom and Dad, in our room.

Page 18

Your Dad is a music lover and he played his favorite opera songs for you. I rocked you to sleep every night. Here is a picture of you sleeping on my shoulder.

Soon Grandma Haney, Aunt Inez, and cousins Susan, David, and Donald all came to town for a special day. Do you know what that special day was?

It was time to go and see the Judge to sign the adoption papers!

Page 19

The whole Corbett clan came to court with us. Judge Craven asked your dad and I if we would love you and take good care of you for the rest of our lives. We said, "Yes, yes, yes!" Hooray, Hooray, Hooray!

Nicole, this is the story of your birth and adoption. I'm sure that you will treasure many other stories as you grow up. Your parents love to take photos, so you will always have pictures to remind you.

Page 20

[Title Page—a perfect place for child input! Let your child help select decorations and pictures.]

Fall is a wonderful time of year. The leaves start to turn colors, and children go back to school. Families think about the holidays.

Something else happened one fall, on October 13, 1995. Manny, can you guess what that is? Let me give you a hint. Someone you know very well was born on this day.

You!

You were born at 6:45 AM on October 13, 1995. That is the day we call your birthday. You see, Manny, everyone in the world starts by getting born. You, too!

Before you were born you grew in a special place under your first mother's tummy. Sandra is the name of your first mother. She gave you your birthday. Sometimes we call her Mommy Sandra or your Birthday Mom.

[Insert birth certificate.]

Manny, it takes two people, a man and a woman, to make a baby. Everyone in the world starts with a birthmother and a birthfather. You, too.

We don't know very many facts about your birthfather. Not even his name. Some things we will have to guess at. I wonder, does he like computers as much as you?

Remember, Manny, much of how you look comes from your birth parents. I wonder, do you look like your birth father? Since we don't have a picture of him, use your imagination and draw a picture of what you think he looks like.

Manny, after you were born, your birthmother was very happy to have given birth to such a lovely baby. But she was also very sad and confused. Part of the reason she was sad was that she had some big problems. We can talk more about them when you are a little older. Sandra couldn't take care of you or of any baby. What was she going to do?

The people at the hospital decided that Mommy Sandra needed extra help to take care of you. They called the Department of Family and Children's Services and asked if your family could have its own social worker.

A social worker is someone whose job it is to keep children safe.

Karen was the name of your first social worker. She visited your house to watch your family and make sure you were healthy and happy. She came to your house a lot. She was worried that your mother slept all the time and was very sad. No one changed your diapers or fixed your bottles. After all, that's a parent's job.

Even though Mommy Sandra had trouble taking care of you, the social worker said that she was a "nice person."

Karen says that Mommy Sandra likes to read books. Sandra's favorite food is pizza. Her ethnicity is part African American and part Portuguese. She is "a tall, slim woman," says Karen.

Karen decided to write a letter to the Judge about your family. A Judge is a man or woman who is a very smart and wise person. People visit the Judge and explain their problems. They ask the Judge for help with decisions. Your social worker told the Judge, "Manny's Mom is very sad and having a hard time keeping him healthy and safe." The Judge decided that you needed to live in a foster home.

A foster home is a safe place where children live until they either return to their first parents or move into an adoptive home. Manny, your social worker brought you to your first foster home one cold winter day. You stayed in this home for three years. You called your foster mother Aunty Beverly and had an old dog named Ginger.

Sandra was sad because her brain needed a special medicine that a doctor prescribes. Sandra didn't like going to the doctor and often didn't take her special medicine. Her sadness was not your fault. You were just a little baby.

Each month the social worker met with Mommy Sandra. She tried to help your mother make changes so she could take good care of you. But it was just too hard. Little was different from when you first entered foster care, and three years is such a long time to wait.

It became time for the social worker to make a new plan. That plan was called adoption.

What is adoption? Adoption is when a little boy or girl grows up with a different family than their birth family.

Children by birth and children by adoption depend on their parents to take care of them until they can take care of themselves. Even though children come into families in different ways, the end result is the same: We are all family. And no matter how a child joins a family, that child is loved bunches and bunches.

The social worker talked to Aunty Beverly and Uncle Jeff about your adoption plan. She said, "Do you think you would want to take excellent care of Manny and always love him?"

Guess what, Manny? They said, "Yes, we would love to be Manny's forever family!"

A family is two or more people who usually live in the same house (but not always) and who love each other a lot. Some families are small and some are really big. Some children grow up with one parent, either a mom or a dad. Other families have grandparents who are taking care of their grandchildren.

Manny, remember that families are about how you feel on the inside, not how you look on the outside.

Page 17

After you had been living with your family for a while, it was time to visit the Judge to have your adoption made official. Remember, a Judge is a person whose job it is to make decisions about people's lives.

Once you were in the Judge's room, the process didn't take very long. The Judge decided, "Yes, this is in the best interest of this child." She signed the papers and you became adopted.

Page 18

Everyone in the courtroom was sooo happy. I bet they wanted to yell, "Hip-hip-hooray!"

Congratulations, Manny!

Page 19

4.

MAKING AN ADOPTION LIFEBOOK

Now you are ready to assemble the Lifebook. Your information is as complete as possible. The time is right. The text is written.

Materials (*all* materials used should be nontoxic):

* **three-ring binder or album (size is up to you) containing page protectors (acid free)**
* **photos**
* **construction paper (acid free)**
* **stickers (see Kids Like Me section), glue, glitter**
* **rubber-stamps**

Don't use anything unless it says "acid free." "Archivally safe" is like "lite" or "reduced calorie"—not a term I would trust. If it's acid free, then the manufacturer will want to proudly list that information.

If the Lifebook is for an infant, then make sure the pages are brightly decorated. But do not use glitter or paste or anything that you don't want going into their mouths!

One practical idea for toddlers is to laminate the pages. Use a wire binding to hold them together, and be sure all edges are smooth. Then—ta-da!—it's a worry free Lifebook.

Some people purchase very expensive and fancy Lifebook covers. Choose your albums carefully. The entire point of a Lifebook is that people will read it to their children (who then might read it to the next generation). A successful Lifebook is worn, ripped, and stained. It doesn't work if it is a work of art and you are afraid of getting it dirty. I recommend "pretty" but not too fancy—your choice.

Scrapbooking: This is a perfect chance for you to combine your special talents and skills in a timeless gift for your child. Go ahead and create your Lifebook with the die-cuts, stenciling, and fancy journaling tools that are available.

Scrapbooking requires hours. You may find that this enterprise serves as an excellent tool for working with your child and that the craft part serves as a pleasant distraction. Or it may seem just too much to combine with writing the actual text. It won't take long for you to figure out what works for you.

Regardless of what type of book you purchase, copy the pages.

One copy will be for safekeeping; if the adoptee wishes, this can be passed down to future generations—or one could be used for everyday purposes. And as discussed earlier, select pages can be put together for a travel Lifebook.

You can do the entire text on a computer or by hand. Make sure your handwriting is readable, however. There is a certain comfort to having it on the computer. You are able to take a break and later make changes without redoing the entire page.

Try and have one main theme for each page, and keep your text short. If you have a computer, decorate the pages with colorful graphics. If your child is helping out, you might consider using stickers.

You certainly have worked hard to get to this point. Take your completed pages and insert them into the page protectors. Take a deep breath. You are almost done with a seemingly never-ending task. Congratulations!

Caution: It is tempting to select decorations which solely reflect your child's cultural background. Does a five -year-old want cultural stickers or Dora? Blues Clues or tasteful grown up stickers? Think about it.

You can have one page per sheet protector or put in two back-to-back. Take pictures of yourself making the Lifebook. (Invest in Kodak, because you will forever be behind the camera!)

Keep each page short and sweet. (Are you tired of hearing this reminder?) Kids normally have a short attention span. Adoption issues can make that span even shorter. This is fine. Take it one page at a time.

If you are making the Lifebook for an infant, you will acquire years of practice. Your child will never have to be "told"—what a luxury. You have years without those unexpected questions, those queries of "Why?"

Your child will be so matter-of-fact by the time s/he turns 4; adoption will be very ordinary and easy to discuss. "Boring," as one 7 year old informed me as we went over his Lifebook. He just wanted more stories about what he was eating as a toddler.

A. Always Make Copies of the Lifebook!

If you are working on a computer, use your Save button often, and put your work on a disk. Writing is a big enough project without losing your work of art in a power surge or the freaky electric storm.

Copy the entire Lifebook. You can go to some place like Staples and they will do it for you in color. The additional cost is well worth it.

You want your child to feel totally safe carrying around this treasured object, like a worn blankie. You also want to be prepared in case they have a major temper tantrum and end up demolishing the Lifebook.

I believe that the Lifebook should be protected and preserved by the adult. Keep an eye on it, but don't make it too difficult to access. Never leave the Lifebook with the child until there is a second copy.

B. Don't Wait for Questions

Children have trouble formulating questions to ask about birthfamily or adoption. Too often, I hear parents say, "Well, I asked them if they had any questions, and they said no." Of course they don't have questions—they don't know where to begin (like me when I first started on the computer). Plus they pick up on the underlying energy involved. Make it easy for them to look at their Lifebooks. They shouldn't have to ask.

Back in the 50s the prevailing wisdom was that parents should minimize adoption discussion. The experts believed that children adopted as infants didn't have "adoption issues." To their credit, my parents gave me a copy of The Chosen Baby and read it to me when I was 4.

In addition, they never kept my adoption a secret. However, as I was growing older, I would have preferred to discuss all aspects of my adoption more freely. What I would have really relished, especially as I got to be a teenager, is an adoption Lifebook. It would have given me a place to start conversations and to invite the whole topic of adoption without feeling that I was somehow hurting my parents' feelings.

The ultimate magic to creating a treasured adoption Lifebook is to start it, work on it as a family, and give it to your child. Even if your Lifebook has five pages, it is tangible proof to your adopted child that s/he is precious enough to deserve this life treasure.

Lifebook Resources (no Cost)

Beth O'Malley's Website: http://www.adoptionlifebooks.com
Tons of free resources. Articles. Monthly newsletter. Success stories. Q &A section. schedule for Beth's live presentations. Plus the LifeBook Shoppe (books, workbooks & special E-reports)

Time Capsule Website: http://dmarie.com/timecap/step1.asp
Discover what happened the day you were born. Headlines, toys, movies, or even famous people born on same date. Free

FREE Scrapbook pages http://www.scrapbookscrapbook.com
This site offers pages and designs you can print out, plus tips for beginners, money saving tips and more. Asian scrapbook design available as well.

Day of Birth http://www.dayofbirth.co.uk/
Learn what day of the week you were born on. Discover how many days until your next birthday, how many seconds old you are. Plus other links. Free

Behind the Name http://www.behindthename.com
Want to know what a name means? From anywhere in the world? This unique site has great articles, tools and links. Free

Birthday Weather http://www.underground.com/
Find the weather for any state or country. If you want weather for a historical date i.e. your child's birthday, Go to that country/city you want, enter that date. Free

Resources for lifebooks seem to come and go. If all else fails go to www.google.com and type in search terms such as ' lifebook supplies' 'adoption stickers' etc. Meantime, here are some tried and true sites:

www.scrapandtell.com— Always something new. Check out the sample adoption page layouts. Attractive with nice wording. Wide selection of adoption/scrapbook supplies.

www.adoptshoppe.com—The Internet's most complete selection of lifebooks, memory books and unique adoption gifts. A trusted site.

www.stickerplanet.com—1 800 557-8678 Call for a catalog.
 I love their diverse multicultural "kid" stickers

www.crayolastore.com— Multicultural crayons & markers. Perfect for helping children better explore their identity and ethnicity.

www.asiathreads.com—Unique China Lifebook resource; Asia Threads conducts projects to obtain pictures of various orphanages and places where children were found in China.

www.fosterclub.com — One of my favorites! A website just for older kids in foster care. (10 and up) Plus a grown up section.

www.adoptionclubhouse.org— Sponsored by the National Adoption Center, this kid-friendly website offers: Kids stories and poems, famous people (who were adopted), message board,
school projects, and a 'grade your parents section.'

Favorite Children's Adoption & Foster Care Books

<u>The Family Book</u> by Tom Parr (ages 2 plus) My latest discovery. Eye catching, colorful illustrations. Funny text explains it's normal for families to be different. Universal appeal

<u>Wise Up Power Book</u> by Marilyn Schoettle (ages 5 plus) Need help with answering race/adoption questions? This unique resource helps adopted and foster kids handle a variety of common questions.

<u>Rosie's Family: An Adoption Story</u> by Lori Rosove (ages 4 plus) Rosie is a beagle who was adopted by schnauzers. She feels different from the rest of her family and sets forth many questions that children who were adopted may have.

<u>A Mother for Choco</u> by Keiko Kasza (ages 2–8) A little yellow bird is in search of his mother. Mrs. Bear doesn't look like him, but she hugs, kisses, dances, and—most important—loves Choco.

<u>How I Was Adopted</u> by Joanna Cole (ages 4–8) A delightful, interactive story about how "Samantha" was born and adopted. Helps tastefully explain birds and bees and birth.

<u>Forever Fingerprints</u> by Sherrie Eldridge (5 plus) This book will have you laughing while the author gracefully explains the birthing process and the importance of connections with biological family.

<u>Zachary's New Home</u> by Geraldine Blomquist and Paul Blomquist (ages 4–10) Zachary, a little kitten, has to move to a foster home and then gets adopted. Helpful for children in foster care .

Other Books and Resources
By Beth O'Malley M.Ed

Don't forget to sign up for the monthly newsletter! Arriving monthly in your email box are fresh tips, special offers, etc. to help you on your journey. www. adoptionlifebooks.com/signup.htm

<u>My Foster Care Journey</u> (ages 4-8) Ready made, fill-in-the blank lifebook. Perfect for a busy social worker or foster parent. Written in kid friendly terms, this tool supports any permanent goal: guardianship, kinship, return home, as well as adoption

<u>For When I'm Famous: A teen fost/adopt lifebook</u> (ages 9 –15) One of the few "tween" and teen life books. Funny and realistic, this guide helps kids look at their past and future. Helpful for teens ' not interested' in a traditional lifebook.

<u>My Adoption Lifebook: A Workbook for Kids from China</u> by Beth O'Malley (ages 5-8) Interactive & fun, easy way to begin adoption story discussion. Book format makes it 'OK' to talk about inner questions. Designed to be completed with parent and child.

<u>Special Reports</u>: $7 (only available as an E-mail report)
#1. How to Start Your Child's Adoption Lifebook
#2. How to Make Lifebooks: with Adopted Children Ages 5-9
    (International Version)
#3. How to Make Lifebooks: with Adopted Children Ages 5-9
    (Domestic Version)
#4. How to Make Lifebooks: with Babies & Toddlers (inter.& dom)
#5 Waiting Parents & Lifebooks: What You Need to Know
(inter& dom)

order online at www. adoptionlifebooks.com